Baby Moses in a basket,
floating down the Nile.
Baby Moses in a basket,
slowly sailing for a while.

Curious Ibis, in the water,
comes to take a closer peek,
sees a baby, little baby,
kicking tiny baby feet.

Basket drifting to the shallows
catches near the reedy shore.
Gently, Ibis sets it free
to sail a while more.

Among the boats and floating barges
past the green papyrus reeds,
Baby Moses on a voyage
where the river Nile leads.

Mama Hippo, like a mountain,
rises upward from the deep,
follows Baby, Baby Moses,
as he dozes off to sleep.

Mama Hippo nudges softly,
helps the basket skim along,
watching over Baby Moses
so that nothing will go wrong.

Little baby sweetly dreaming,
Mama Hippo as his guide,
down the river, through fast currents,
basket rocking side to side.

High above, the storm clouds gather
up beyond the swelling Nile.
Far below, from river's bottom
rises Mighty Crocodile.

Swiftly gliding, steering Baby,
thrashing through the seething storm,
keeping Baby, Baby Moses,
snug and safe, dry and warm.

Whirling water swirling round them,
currents roaring even more,
plunging through the wild waters
toward the calm of sandy shore.

Baby Moses in a basket
floats among the reeds and flowers
near the pharaoh's daughter, bathing
in the pale good-morning hours.

Baby Moses stirs and whimpers
in his basket on the Nile.

"What? A baby! Oh, sweet baby!"
cries the maiden with a smile.

Up she lifts him, full of wonder.
"I drew you from the river deep.
You are safe now in my arms—
close your eyes, go back to sleep."